MANDALA

COLORING BOOK FOR STRESS REFIEF

VOL.3

ADULT COLORING BOOK DESIGNS

COLOR TEST PAGE

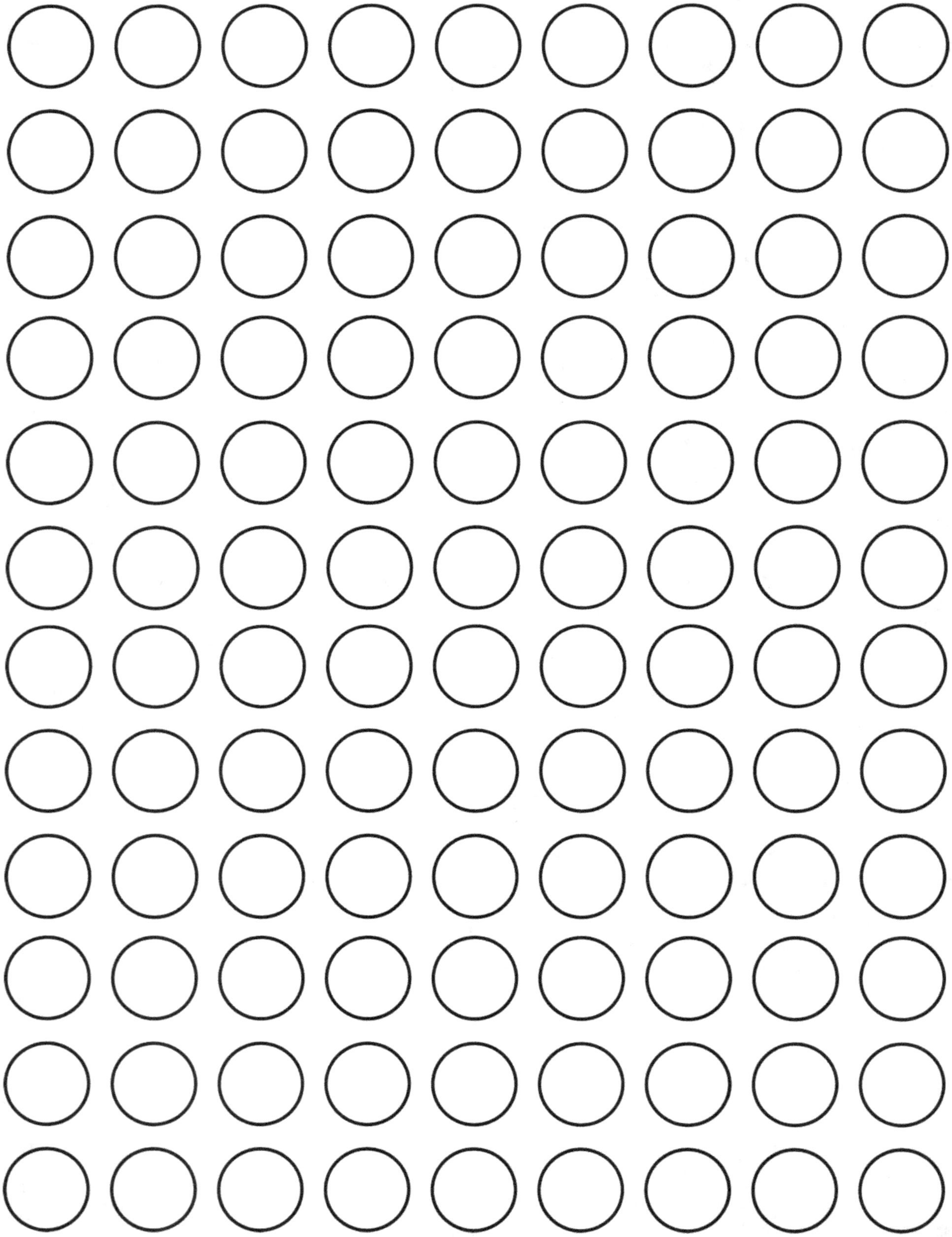

COLOR TEST PAGE

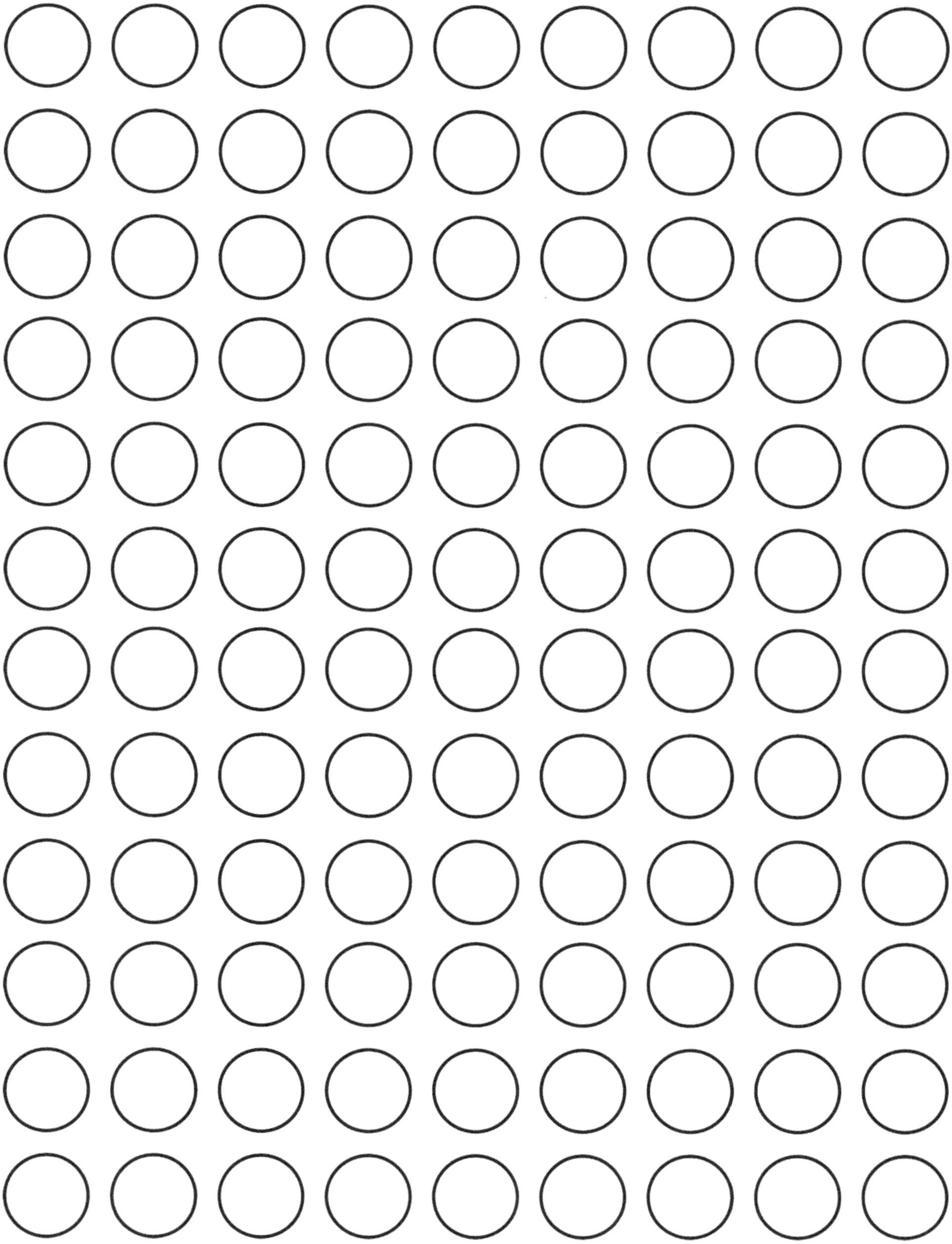

www.ingramcontent.com/pod-product-compliance
Lightning Source LLC
Chambersburg PA
CBHW080551190526
45169CB00007B/2723
* 9 7 8 1 5 3 9 4 7 2 0 7 0 *